Protecting Seniors' Wealth Guide

Guidelines; Facts; Plans of Action; and Reasons for Protecting Seniors, Their Wealth, and Your Inheritance

Anne McGowan

Consulting Lawyer:
James Kelly, LL.B

Blue Sea Publishing
Langley, Washington USA

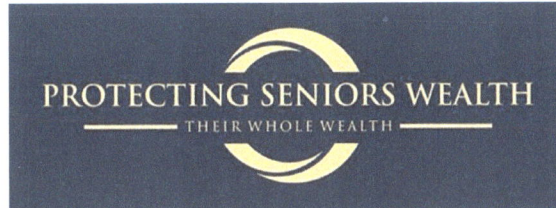

What People Are Saying About the Website and Protecting Seniors' Wealth

An important read and practical guide for anyone with elderly family members. Anne shines a light on an unfortunately all too familiar problem that will potentially expand as our countries demographics continue to shift towards the older end of the spectrum. She offers excellent advice and practical ways to ensure that our most important people are safe from financial harm.

– Jason Reynolds, Director at Action Wealth,
Financial Advisor, Melbourne, Australia

As an ending full-time carer for my late mother, I am chuffed to see your site. Only last night, I have found out that family have lost some inheritance due to dubious family members".

– Linda Daniel JP, Editor at Soul Editing, Australia

Published in the United States by Blue Sea Publishing

Cover design: Anne McGowan
Interior design and Editor: Janet Foster, Blue Sea Publishing
Graphic design: Paul Fitz-Patrick, WinWin Internet Solutions

ISBN: 978-0-9963438-5-5

15 14 13 12   4 3 2 1
1st edition, November 2015

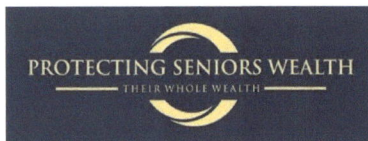

www.protectingseniorswealth.com.au
Phone: +61 2 6577 5560
Postal Address: PO Box 1015
Singleton NSW 2330, Australia

Contents

Our lives begin to end the day we become silent about things that matter.

– Martin Luther King

Notes from the Author

• Overview

Heading off elder financial abuse, could be one of the most important things you do in your life! If you suspect financial abuse of some sort, that could be or is taking place concerning an elderly person in your life, never doubt your suspicions and be vigilant in looking into it. To some extent we have a moral responsibility to assist if we can.

Financial abuse of the elderly is much more widespread than we are aware of and a recent media interview indicated a rise of 20 percent. When this happens to an elderly person, they are more than upset. They feel deeply hurt, humiliated and distressed. It's called "The Ultimate Betrayal" with good reason.

It occurs in different ways: manipulation, passive aggressive behaviour, verbal abuse or even physical abuse. Usually it is people they know who commit this form of crime and make no mistake, these people do not care about the wellbeing of the elderly. They are only interested in getting the assets or the money.

Unfortunately, when this is done to an elderly person, they are too embarrassed and humiliated, or feel too vulnerable to speak of it either in private or publicly. One of the main reasons they are reluctant to talk about it and take action is because one or more family members are often the perpetrators.

Yes, our research into this indicates it is most often a family member. Though it also could be a carer or caregiver, a friend, or someone posing as a Financial Advisor. Elderly people do often need additional care and assistance with their affairs as they become older and there are many good well trained people to assist with elder care. However, do "keep your eyes open", do take action if there are "signs", detailed more so in this guide.

There's one more thing that's important to bear in mind if you're the one looking out for an elderly person, a tactic these particular type of people may use is to try to discredit you. They can carry out defamatory behaviour targeted at you.

Know this, it's for a reason, to get you "out of the way", so they can gain access to the elderly person, then the assets. My advice is to trust your instincts, don't let these people who commit these "low acts" undermine your confidence, and proceed to step-in, do whatever you can and take appropriate action.

It can be a process, short or lengthy, and is sometimes complicated, depending on the circumstances. We have outlined the varying courses of action in the coming pages. At the time, when I experienced this, I found it difficult to comprehend the enormity of what was occurring. To be honest, I wasn't really aware this happened to the extent it does, or prepared to be able to deal with it effectively. I hope the guidelines here make it easier for others to work out "what to do". Not always, but often, taking action quickly is imperative.

Introduction

• Who Do You Contact First?

This book is for seniors wanting to ensure they're wealth remains intact, and for people who are looking to assist elderly people to do the same – protect them and their wealth.

It's a good idea if you can, to plan ahead to head off such a situation where "wealth abuse" could possibly occur. Planning ahead and making sure Wills are completed, and checked, to ensure they're thorough is one of the first things to do. However, in some cases you may need to be more involved, you may be required to take more action, legal or otherwise.

The World Health Organisation considers people over the age of 55 as seniors. If you haven't already done so by this time, consider getting your affairs "in order". It is wise to consult with **your Lawyer, your Accountant and Financial Advisor,** to check everything is up to date.

If you're reading this or having concerns about your senior parents or elderly people close to you, if you have "nagging recurring thoughts" about their well-being and wealth protection, chances are your concerns are real and it would be a good idea to at least be informed and prepared. You may need to take action quickly or over a period of time.

In any case, being informed is key, it can save precious time and mean the difference in being successful or not.

Please Note: We do strongly advise people, to seek professional help in the first instance, if they suspect wealth abuse, as laws can vary from State to State in each country.

However, this book could be a most useful reference for ideas to assist with the process of protecting a person or a family's wealth. It could help to safeguard the whole wealth of an individual or a family. Sometimes action needs to be taken promptly, other times action is taken over time.

If there is something we have not included in this reference book, that you feel may help others, please email any details you have to us. We will do our best to add it, as it may be of assistance to someone else.

Certain suggestions have been repeated in different sections of this Guide.

We have done this for those who may need a quick reference to parts of the publication, to ensure crucial information is not missed. However we do recommend reading the whole publication, if possible, to be fully informed.

Why Be Aware of This Topic?

• The Importance of "Being Aware"

This book has been constructed to provide guidelines for "what to do" to prevent the abuse of the elderly for their money or wealth. Awareness is key and if people have some knowledge on the subject, including the "warning signs", they could be in a better position to prevent it happening.

If you're fortunate enough to have family who are caring and supportive good people, who function with integrity, that's great! Unfortunately, many people simply are unaware of the high rate of elder financial abuse. One recent media interview spoke of how elder financial abuse has increased and they mentioned the statistics show a rise of 20 percent in 2014 alone – that is huge!

Many people simply don't realise this is something you need to consider, and they may have no idea how to deal with it as their parents age. Elder abuse for their money, their wealth, their assets, happens a lot! If you speak with Real Estate Agents, Lawyers, Investors and Bank Employees on the subject, you will most likely hear comments such as, "Oh, this happens all the time"! or "Yes, it happens, and it's not good when it does".

It appears that although a majority of us wouldn't dream of doing anything like this, there are many who would and they would carry this out often without being noticed, until it's too late. That is, real estate may have been sold or legal documents may have been signed without the elderly people realising what they actually signed, or they are abused verbally, or something we all hope wouldn't happen, even abused physically as well to sign legal documents.

Until the laws change to further protect our seniors or the elderly, it's a good idea to be aware and take steps to protect their wellbeing, their whole wealth, and quite possibly you could find you're protecting your inheritance as well. For the senior people concerned here, it's about preserving the way of life they choose to have in their later years, and that's important to maintain it for them.

It's also about looking out for our elders, looking for signs of them being unusually upset or signs of confusion in detail. Our elders can feel vulnerable in their later years, and they certainly become fearful and actually do fear the perpetrators, the one's conducting financial abuse. The loss of a person's dignity as a result is a huge factor, we cannot emphasise this enough.

You may find you're doing this to protect your inheritance that your parents have already decided to leave you, or you simply wish to prevent this undesirable behaviour happening to your lovely parents or someone you are close to. If you're looking for the motivation to take action, imagine how horrible that would feel to realise these precious elderly people we know and love became the subject of such abuse or manipulation.

Sadly, many realise financial abuse may be happening all too late. In fact by this time efforts to take legal action can be made more difficult. Possibly the ageing parents have already experienced coercion, have been manipulated or verbally abused to sign documents. Consider this scenario for a moment; if that isn't upsetting enough for the elderly, imagine how they would then feel when the reality sinks in – they have not only literally lost their wealth, but their means to support their lifestyle, they experience loss of dignity, independence and freedom to choose, and they have also lost the inheritance they planned to bequeath, it has literally all been signed over to unscrupulous people, possibly even other so-called family members. It would be devastating.

It's something to remember, these people who commit these low acts against the elderly, may have used passive aggressive bullying tactics, in order to get what they wanted – the money and the property. If it has already occurred, do consider being supportive to the elderly person that this happened to and see what can be done to assist them.

This is why this Guide was produced to help others be more effective to actively step in to protect the elderly, and ensure these elder people actually do enjoy their later years in life, with their dignity and wealth in tact to continue to support them. It is for this very reason, heading off elder financial abuse, could be one of the most important things you do in your life.

Financial fraud is also elder abuse. Considering older people in most countries control an estimated 70 percent of the wealth, this makes them a prime target. To help put this in perspective, surveys conducted in recent years in the Unites States alone, indicates elders have lost billions of dollars to financial fraud and many millions of elders were victims of financial swindling. Considering this, the occurrence rate worldwide would of course be much higher, possibly even making them our most exploited citizens.

A Guide for What to Do

• What are The Steps to Take?

Contact Your Lawyer for Advice

Each situation can vary, with a range of different circumstances, in addition to the laws varying in each State and Country. Therefore it is most important to consult with your Lawyer in the first instance, to choose an appropriate course of action. Plus it's a good time to begin briefing your Lawyer, as you may at any time need assistance to step in quickly.

If you do not have a Lawyer who is competent in these matters, one who is interested in assisting you and with experience in Elder Law, there is a listing of competent firms and their Lawyers who specialise in Elder Law on our website. Their names and contact details are also shown, it's all on the Links page. These firms work in the area of Elder Law. There are Links included that can take you directly to their own website home pages.

It is important to work with a local Lawyer who works in the area of Elder Law.

Contact Your Accountant or Financial Adviser

If you suspect fraudulent activity either has or could be about to occur, it's important to notify the Accountant, Financial Advisor or the Investment Institution concerned.

You may be placed in a situation where you're caring for an elderly person, or possibly assisting a senior person with their affairs – their financial arrangements, including their investments. If you notice a number of unaccounted for large regular withdrawals, or one or more large withdrawals, it could be wise to check with the appropriate organisation. They will know what to do.

The reason why it's important to notify the banking or investment organisation is they may be able to put a "flag" or a "stop" on the account. This then gives you valuable time to look into the possible suspicious activity, plus to obtain records of the transactions and to take legal action if need be. If the withdrawals are suspicious, contact your Lawyer immediately, if you have not done so already.

Contact your Financial Institution

Contact the Bank or Credit Union or other Financial Banking Institution where the person you are assisting, has their accounts. It could be best to go in personally if you can, if not call them. Explain that you think someone is accessing their Bank Accounts, or they are about to do so.

You will need to identify yourself by stating your name and your relationship to the person you are assisting. They may ask if you have a Power of Attorney for this person, or if you have permission from the concerned person in writing. If you do not have either, they may ask if it's possible to take the elder person along with you if they are able to.

There are staff employed there who are trained to deal with such situations. In some cases they may take you to a private room to look at the Bank Accounts, subject to privacy laws. Remember to take your Power of Attorney with you if you have one.

If you have a Power of Attorney (or equivalent in other States and Countries), check with the bank or investment institution that your POA has been properly lodged with that banking organisation. If you have not already done so, you may need a signature from a Lawyer's office, stating that it's a certified copy of the original document.

When you arrange for a certified copy of the original document to be signed, you may want to ask for two or three copies, so that one can be provided to an investment advisor for lodgement in their files and one could be kept for another purpose that may arise.

The banking institutions need to receive this copy so they can have it on file, process it to acknowledge it on their records. It's important this is done in order for the Banking or Financial Institution to take action if required.

Many people have a Power of Attorney drawn up, so that it can be used when required at some stage in the future. However, they may not know that the banks need to sight it and register it on their records when it's actually required for a banking transaction.

Check the Bank Statements

Ensure you keep any Bank Statements you may have. If you already have records of transactions, look at them, check to make sure they're in order. Look for any suspicious activity such as larger than usual withdrawals over a period of time, or for any large unusual withdrawals.

In some cases, depending on the State or Country you reside in, if money has been withdrawn, after you lodged your concerns, after you've advised the Bank of possible fraudulent activity, it can be their responsibility to recover the funds. Usually though these institutions will do their best to assist accordingly.

If you suspect money has been illegally withdrawn, either by someone forging a signature, or the elderly person you are helping, has been coerced or abused to sign, notify your Lawyer immediately, compile the records, and act on your Lawyer's advice promptly.

If you have actual proof of money being taken, your Lawyer may suggest legal action, depending on the amount, or may suggest further monitoring.

Legal action regarding misappropriation of funds could mean either a letter from the Lawyer, action to recover the funds, or possibly an application to a Court (the name of this Court in each State or Country is often different).

Keep Records

Keep all records you may have, including:

> Bank Statements,
>
> Correspondence,
>
> Doctor's Contact Details,
>
> Medical Reports or Recommendations and Referrals, even Test Results, as any of these details could be required at some point.

Note: Never deal in cash transactions where there is no paper trail. Instead be able to provide some paperwork to establish the transactions.

Keep a Diary

Write everything down in a diary or notebook, including the date, the name of the person you spoke to, and details of the discussion or appointment. You may need to refer to this later, or possibly offer this as proof during a meeting, or in some cases if it proceeds to a hearing in a court or tribunal.

Do You Need To Take Action Quickly?

• Six Things That Can Occur

THIS IS IMPORTANT

The diagram below lists where and when different types of abuse can be experienced by seniors as they age and become frailer.

If you notice or suspect any of the following types of abuse, or difficulties developing regarding an elderly person's health, there are things you can do to take action. They are addressed further on the following pages.

• How You Take Action If the Following Occurs

Money Taken from Bank Accounts

If you think this is or may be occurring, do not hesitate to assist by contacting the bank concerned. Explain the situation. Employees at banks are trained to assist with such matters. If you find someone that isn't, they will be happy to ask someone else who is to come and assist you.

As one bank employee stated, when Anne went to the bank to inquire about this, when she apologised because it was not a pleasant matter, the bank employee said to her reassuringly "this happens a lot".

Note to Reader: When looking at this, keep in mind, if someone is planning to take the wealth of an elderly person, they may have been looking at "how" they could do this for some time. They may have already taken steps to do this or may already be taking money from their accounts.

— The Role a Bank Can Play

A bank can help you *look at Bank Account Transactions and obtain Financial Statements and Data.*

- The bank's staff will inform you of what they can do to help, depending on your particular situation.

- The extent could depend on whether you have legal documents.
- What they can do is subject to privacy laws.

6 Things That Can Occur

Money Taken From Bank Accounts	Assets Being Sold
Signs of Dementia or No Longer Capable of Managing Their Affairs	Coercion or Abuse To Sign Legal Documents
Passive Aggressive or Abusive Behaviour For Money	What Can I Do If They Are In Hospital Care

— The Role a Tribunal or Court Can Play

- A Tribunal or Court has the power *to stop a property sale.*

- The Tribunal or Court also has the power to instruct a bank *to freeze a Bank Account and place a Stop or Hold on the Account's Transactions.*

- They have the power to *order a review of the Bank Accounts.*

— It's Important to Note the Following:

- Before a Tribunal or Court can act and take action, they do need some proof that a property is about to be sold.

- They will also require medical evidence, regarding the elderly person's "decision-making" capabilities, in one form or another.

- You can however, if you need to move quickly, if the sale of the house is underway, or money is being taken from the Bank Accounts, you can advise them of this and they may decide to begin the process.

- They have trained people who will work with you, inform you what you need to do, possibly provide you with a contact and a reference number. It could be possible for you to then supply them with the other information they may require, such as a letter from a Doctor or proof of an imminent property sale when you obtain it.

Note to Reader: The Doctor's letter and confirmation the Court or Tribunal require does need to be provided before they can actually take action. Once they have it, they can also conduct a hearing.

You can work with your Lawyer who will do this for you, complete the application and lodge it with the Tribunal, or you can complete this in conjunction with your Lawyer's help, or complete it yourself.

Assets Being Sold

- If you suspect the Assets, such as the house, are being sold or they're going to try, there are a number of things to do.

- Contact the real estate agents in the area, mention your concerns, and ask if they have been approached to do an appraisal, or handle the sale or perhaps an Auction.

- Ensure you leave them with "your contact details" and ask them to contact you if they hear anything.
- Specify this could result in legal action should the sale of the property proceed. Most are only too happy to be of assistance, as they don't like this either. But for the odd one, it won't hurt to mention it.

When doing this don't give up, often after a few phone calls to the Real Estate Agents, one will say, "That property sounds familiar, let me look at my file". Another said, "Yes, I was asked to give an appraisal, let me look at the details of who asked for it". They will usually be happy to cooperate and give you the details. Most agents don't like this behaviour. You may even hear them say something like this, "Unfortunately this happens all the time".

If the Real Estate Agent is already engaged to sell the house, do contact your Lawyer immediately. That may be able to intervene with a legal letter, and that may be all you need.

However, if that is not enough to deter them, they may suggest an application to a Court or Tribunal. Either can step in, it depends on the circumstances. It's a matter of time, the details of what has occurred, and if you have proof. A description of each organisation appears later in this guide.

Note to Reader: The "key" to preventing something like this happening is to take action, and often this needs to be done quickly. *Lodging a caveat* is a way to protect an estate or interest in land against some other dealing, such as a transfer or mortgage. If you're unsure about this, you should seek legal advice.

> **Example:** One story told to Anne was about how a man had stepped in just in time before one of his siblings sold their elderly parent's house. They did manage to stop the sale of the house. Keeping the house was what the parents actually wanted, before they had been persuaded and manipulated to sell it.

When Hospitalised

If you suspect abuse of any sort, including financial abuse, is occurring and the elderly person is in hospital or has been hospitalised for any reason, *contact the Social Worker.*

The Social Worker employed by the hospital, has been trained to deal with this type of situation and they can help you. Ring the hospital, ask for the name of their Social Worker, or the equivalent, and contact them immediately.

It's important they are notified straight away. They may be able to take certain action to assist, if they are notified in time.

Explain the circumstances, there are things they have the power to do, such as extend a person's stay in hospital where they will be safe, until the matter is addressed. They can advise their staff to watch over the patient.

In a Care Facility or In-Home Nursing Agency

If the elderly person is residing in a Care Facility, ask to speak with the Manager and inform them of your concerns. They are trained to assist with these matters.

If an In-Home Nursing Agency has been engaged to care for an elderly person in some capacity, contact the Agency and ask to speak to the Manager. Advise them who you are, if they don't know you already, the reason you're concerned and what course of action you're taking and why.

Keep them updated. They can make a note on their files so that their nursing staff can be aware of the situation. They can communicate with the elderly person's Doctor. Some Doctors can and do request a Registered Nurse from a Nursing Agency to visit the home regularly, if they have concerns about a patient's well-being.

It's helpful to write down the details of all your contacts and the conversations briefly, as you may need to refer to these notes.

Aggressive Conduct Towards the Elderly

The elderly person's Doctor can help. Contact the Doctor and explain what is occurring or your concerns, it's important to advise them of the details.

There are a couple of things they can do and their involvement is sometimes important. They can provide a letter, as mentioned in the previous point, for the Tribunal. They can also lodge a Request for a Registered Nurse to visit on a regular basis to check on the elderly person.

- **Coercion or Abusive Behaviour to Change Wills or Power of Attorney**

If the elderly person is not of sound mind or has become intimidated or afraid of the abuser, they may just go along with the abuser. They might decide, for a number of reasons, to simply give up because they can't take it anymore. They could also decide to agree and cooperate with the abuser, because they're frightened of what they might do to them, or they just want the abuse to stop, or they're embarrassed, or they are concerned for their health or their safety.

It would be best to consult with your Lawyer, determine the best action to take, proceed without hesitation and quickly.

The Signs Of Coercion

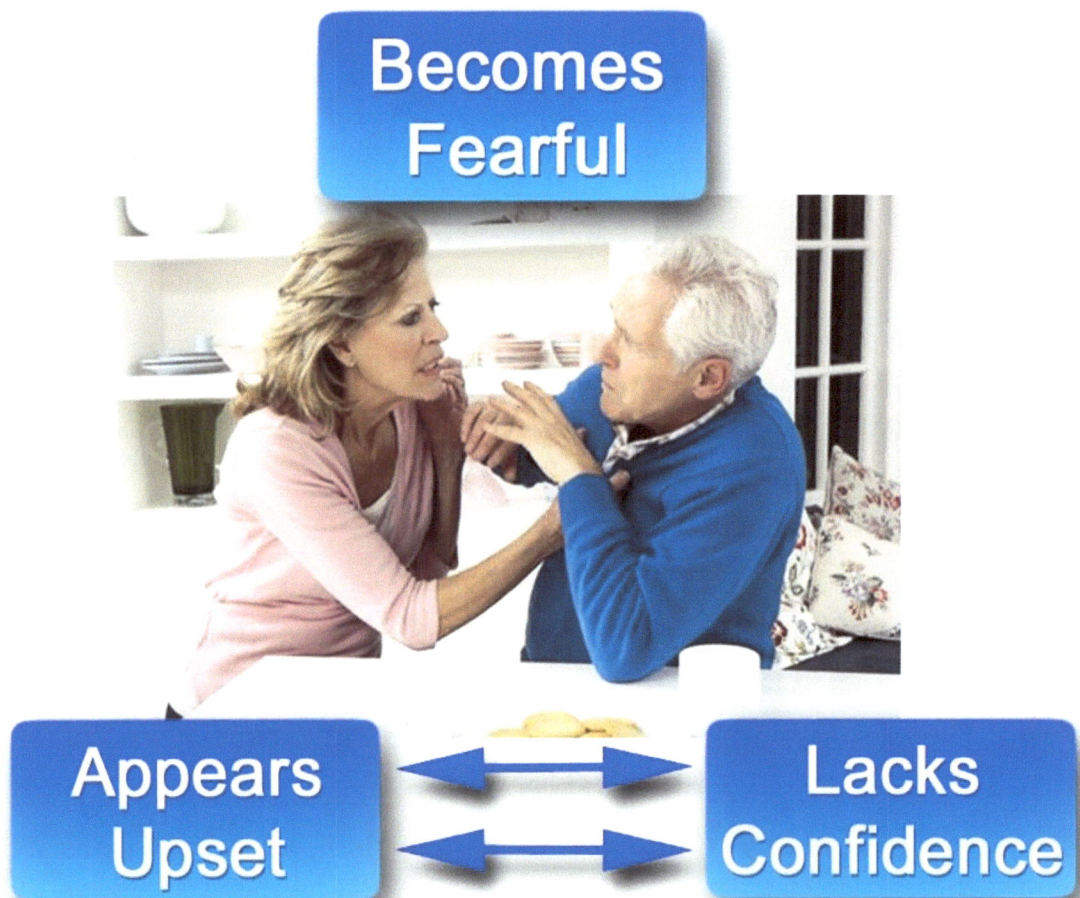

Becomes Fearful

Appears Upset

Lacks Confidence

What Is the Key
to Being Effective?

- ## Seek Good Legal Advice

As you could well imagine, situations such as these are widespread and can vary. The first step is to get good legal advice and if you're not happy with a Lawyer, find one who has experience in this area and who will work with you.

> **Example:** A Lawyer Anne initially went to looking for advice was quite complacent and virtually insinuated there was not a lot that could be done. This actually wasted valuable time. Another Lawyer was found, who was prepared to get involved and try to use the laws and regulations available, to take action and begin proceedings to take legal action. In other words, to do whatever could be done.

If you do not have a Lawyer who can assist you, there is a Listing of Competent Lawyers, with experience in Elder Law, click on the Links page, on our website: www.protectingseniorswealth.com.au.

Important Reasons for Obtaining Legal Advice

We suggest working with a Lawyer for many reasons, and the following describes some examples of legal proceedings in action, and highlights the importance of gaining professional advice and guidance.

- It is worth noting, if an elder person is subjected to pressure to sign a contract or legal document, they may have a cause of action in equity to have the contract set aside. That is, where a contract is found to be entered into as a result of undue influence, this will render the contract voidable.

- Or, if transactions have been imposed upon weak or vulnerable persons that can allow the transactions to be set aside.

Taking Action

• Keeping Records

The thing to do next is to work with your chosen legal representative, and follow their advice. Take action promptly. Engage them to assist you.

In some cases, simply knowing that legal action could and will be taken if necessary, can be enough to deter this sort of behaviour or put a stop to the situation going any further.

Try to find out what exactly is going on and get proof if you can.

If you have proof, a lawyer may suggest taking legal action through the Courts to reverse the transaction and stop further erosion of assets, and make the abuser accountable.

If the evidence is not enough yet, they may suggest a government organisation, a Tribunal, established to assist Senior citizens with such matters. There are specific Tribunals and Courts in each jurisdiction that deal with these matters.

In the first instance, check out the government organisation in your country that helps to step-in with these cases. They will have certain requirements before they can step in. They need proof of certain activities, ask them what they need in order to assist with the situation.

Go through their website to get an understanding of how they work, familiarise yourself with their requirements and procedures. You may need to contact this organisation, ask for advice and even make a submission to them. If you can work with your Lawyer, they can do this for you or you can follow their advice, recommendations and guidance and do it yourself.

Don't be afraid to bring the issue up with bank employees, Real Estate Agents and others as they are used to dealing with this. They may be able to help you with relevant details.

Keep good records as you go:

- Write everything down, including dates and contacts.
- Make file notes of conversations.
- Keep a diary and keep your records, you may need to refer to it and you may need it later.

- Make a checklist and follow through.

- You might find it important to take notes as you proceed. If it becomes complicated or lengthy, you will find it helpful if you can refer to your notes.

Different Organisations That Can Help: Your Government Aged Care Organisation, a Tribunal, a Court

- ## How Can They Help?

Your Government Aged Care Department

Your Aged Care Department in your state or country will have an Aged Care Assessment Team (ACAT) or similar, and they can send a representative, such as a Geriatrician, to the home, to do an ACAT assessment. That's if you don't have one already. They do however require a Doctor's request before they can do so. An Aged Care Assessment (such an ACAT Assessment) may be needed to present to either the Tribunal or the Court.

Tribunal

A Tribunal conducts hearings about adults with a disability relating to making decisions, as they may require a legally appointed decision maker.

Court

A Court has unlimited civil jurisdiction.

   Please Note: Names and contact details for government departments responsible for Aged Care will vary from State to State and Country to Country. We suggest you look on Google for names and contacts details of the organisation in your area. If you do not have access to the Internet perhaps ask someone who does, or check with your Doctor's office or a government department's office nearby, they will be happy to help.

The Different Situations

- ## Important Reasons to Get Involved

What Are the Signs to Look For?

The signs are sometimes subtle, or sometimes more obvious, however it's important you pay attention to them, even if they seem insignificant at the time. There can be a wide range of things to notice:

- Money going missing from Bank Accounts or investment accounts.

- Siblings becoming increasingly rude or begin to demonstrate passive aggressive behaviour towards you for no reason.

- The Elderly ones or your parents start becoming upset or uneasy or confused about detail.

- You notice comments are made about "who should get the inheritance" or similar.

- Money goes missing from the house, or the elderly one makes a comment such as "it has been taken".

- There is no longer enough pension money left to buy good food or personal items.

- Pay attention to your instincts, sometimes the signs are not obvious, however if you get the feeling something is not right, chances are you are correct.

- Often this is a most upsetting experience for an elderly person. It can be quite a shock for them, as the people manipulating, or abusing them in whatever form, are meant to be their family, they're meant to care for them in their older years. Pay attention to the older person's behaviour and comments.

- Take particular notice of the body language of the elderly person, when the person you suspect is in the room with them.

- Older people become vulnerable. They may have several people that they wish to keep "onside" who assist them. If some of those people they rely on threaten to withdraw assistance unless their demands for financial gain are not met, this could be most upsetting for them.

- The new friend who begins interacting with the person, and then comes in and takes over.

Signs of Elder Financial Abuse

Please Note: The content of this guide was prepared to educate people in need of some assistance in this area. It should be used as a practical guide only. Common sense, professional and good legal advice is of the utmost importance.

Ensuring You
Are Effective

Sometimes people don't know where to start or what to do. There may be a couple of things you need to do to ensure you're effective, however in some cases there are many things that need to be considered and possibly acted upon.

The following checklist has been created for you to check that you are taking the correct action for your situation. We do highly recommend that you check with your legal advisor who has experience and expertise in Elder Law as to the appropriate action for your own situation. This list is to give you ideas.

If you find there is something else that can be done that is not on the list, please do take the time to inform us, so that we may update our records to help people in the future, thank you.

There isn't a correct order of priority. It does depend on the circumstances surrounding the situation. One or all of the following may need to be considered:

- Contact your Legal representative and Seek advice

- Decide on what action to take and act on it

- Has there been an ACAT assessment done? (if appropriate)

- Does this need to be taken to Court?

- Do you need to contact a Tribunal?

- Should the Bank be contacted?

- Should the Real Estate Agent be contacted?

- Has the person lost capacity to make decisions for themselves?

- **Important Reasons to Do This**

1. To protect and safeguard your assets or an elderly person's assets.

2. To ensure your freedom, to make your own lifestyle choices, stays intact, now and as you age.

3. To ensure, the people you bequeath your assets to, actually receive them.

4. To maintain the family's wealth and integrity.

5. To ensure the ongoing support for ones "quality of life".

6. To maintain ones respect and dignity.

Summary and Key Contacts

- ## For Additional Information and Updates

Please visit the website below, see Anne's other book *The Ultimate Betrayal ... and Its Triple Whammy Effect,* due to be published August 2015; attend a workshop; or register to receive the updates via the website:
www.protectingseniorswealth.com.au.

- ## A Tribunal

This organisation was established to assist with such matters. If you can't afford legal advice or assistance, this may be your best choice for advice and assistance.

- ## A Court

The Court is another option, depending on your legal advice. Your Lawyer will be able to advise you on the appropriate course of action best for your circumstances.

- ## Law Firms

There's a Listing of Firms, and contact details of Lawyers who specialise or have experience in Elder Law on our website. You will find it on the Links page, and there are links to each Firm's website.
www.protectingseniorswealth.com.au.

- ## Financial Institutions

Financial organisations will be only too happy to help you once you explain your situation, your concerns. They are experienced in this area.

- ## Regularly Updated

This Guide will be updated whenever there is important information that should be included. If you know of other details that will assist people, please submit it to us and we'll consider it for inclusion.

Actual Descriptions
of This Happening,
Plus Links to
Media Interviews

• Convinced to Sign Over Investments

There was an elderly lady who lived in an Aged Care Facility. An individual claiming to be a Financial Advisor, during visits to see someone else, gradually gained this lady's confidence. He convinced her to sign her investments over to him. She did and shortly afterwards when she realised she'd been taken advantage of, she died.

There was an older gentleman who was a returned serviceman, and he was employed as a manager at a local club. Another male employee gradually befriended this man and over time systematically persuaded the older gentleman to change his Will and leave him all his assets, including the large rural property and cash investments. The value of his total assets was considerable. People who lived in the town were very upset that this older man had been manipulated and used for his obvious wealth.

• Passive Aggressive Behaviour to Change Wills

An elderly lady, who began to lose her faculties to some extent in her later years, was passively aggressively abused over time, to sign legal documents. A letter from a Specialist Doctor stated, "…she could easily be coerced to make decisions". Before the assessment however, this lady had been persuaded to sign numerous legal documents, resulting in the loss of a large part of her assets, and the loss of inheritance for other people in the family.

• Verbal Abuse to Sign a Power of Attorney

A kind gentleman, who became frail in his later years, was verbally abused to an extreme extent to sign a legal document. He was unwell at the time and following the initial abuse became intimidated and fearful, and as a result his health began to deteriorate further. He was told lies about the family member he trusted implicitly to help him, further eroding his self-worth. The following times he was told to sign legal documents, he just signed them, because he was frightened and his confidence was undermined. This resulted in the loss of large sums of money, and he was denied his freedom to make his lifestyle choices. They took his bank-books, moved into his house, and took over his life. He was very upset, when he told them to get out, they wouldn't.

• Pushed to Sell the Family Home

One couple as they aged, were increasingly manipulated to sell their home. They loved their home and where they lived, they were happy there and happy with their arrangements. However a couple of family members became increasingly aware of the value of the home. They couldn't wait until the older couple passed to receive their inheritance. An unsavoury character they knew explained to them how to access the assets before the couple died and how to cut off the other sibling from their inheritance. They relentlessly carried out this plan, they didn't care how much they upset this couple in the process, and they succeeded in getting control of the assets.

• Coerced or Manipulated to Sign Over Their Home

A lovely older gentleman, who was leading a happy and active social life, owned and lived in his property. His home had increased in value, however he was low on cash. His adopted son offered to give him some cash, if the older gentleman made him a part owner of the property. The older man agreed and signed a legal document, he trusted his adopted son. It wasn't until some years later, when the older gentleman looked into selling his property, to downsize and pay for care for his increasing health needs, that he became aware he had signed the whole property over to the adopted son. He would become very upset, when he told you of this and he eventually died alone in a war veteran's aged care facility.

- **Being Taken Advantage of – Coerced to Sign for a Home Loan**

An elderly woman, who had been showing signs of the onset of dementia for some time, had very few skills in managing her affairs as her husband had always done this. When her husband passed, she was coerced to sign for a mortgage. As a result, this naïve lady in her late seventies was left paying for the mortgage. Prior to this she was debt free, owned her own home, and had considerable cash to support her for the rest of her life and to bequeath to her loved ones. Due to this financial abuse, this woman was left with only a part share in a house, a mortgage to pay, and very little cash in her Bank Accounts. Her assets were eroded and she didn't seem to fully comprehend how it all happened.

- **Larger Than Usual Withdrawals from Bank Accounts**

A woman in her mid-fifties had been helping her parents with their affairs for many years. They trusted her and she took pride in helping them with whatever they wanted to do. When a family member moved into their house, she became suspicious because her parents seemed upset. She found out her Power of Attorney had been revoked by her parents signing a document that this person had produced. Then immediately following she noticed large withdrawals once or twice a week from their Bank Accounts. She knew her parents just didn't make withdrawals like that or spend that much money, so she immediately sought legal advice and took action.

- **Signatures Forged**

An elderly woman, who began experiencing health problems over a period of time, gave her card willingly to one of her sons to pay for groceries. This particular son then persuaded and manipulated her by saying they would look after her. However, this woman's card was used for much more than the groceries, and the son also paid for his own bills, other living expenses and all his debts from the older woman's Bank Accounts. Due to the older woman not having experience in managing money, as her late husband had always managed their finances, her son over time withdrew a large portion of the money the woman had in her Bank

Accounts. The elderly woman was reasonably wealthy and the amount of money taken overall was considerable.

- ## Unauthorised Withdrawals from Bank Accounts

An older gentleman always trustingly left his bankbook in a place where it was easily seen. When one of his family members turned bad, had financial problems and ran up debt, he advised this person he wasn't giving them any more money as he had already given them a lot over the years. This particular family member had other ideas. They took his bankbook, worked out how to forge his signature and made regular large withdrawals. Eventually, they took the bankbook from him and made sure he didn't speak to anyone about it, and they would always be present when other people visited or when he went to appointments, and they listened to his phone calls.

- ## Elderly Couple Interviewed: Son Took Their Assets

An NBN Television Morning Show, in Australia, called Jump In, aired this interview live about Elderly Financial Abuse on October 6, 2014. The link follows: www.jump-in.com.au/show/mornings/latest/2014/october/elder-abuse/.

- ## Mickey Rooney Interview: He Tells His Story of Financial Abuse

At the age of 90, Mickey Rooney bravely shared his personal story of financial abuse with members of the U.S. Congress and the world. He spoke of the shame and humiliation. This interview was aired on NBC News in the U.S.: www.nbcnews.com/id/41992299/ns/business-consumer_news/t/financial-abuse-costs-elderly-billions/#.VE88TfSUeG.

Scenarios and Ideas to Help Avert Situations or Financial Abuse

- ## Accessing the Bank Accounts

Perhaps a letter from your Lawyer, threatening legal action and notifying the Bank, could prevent any further access.

- ## Taking Valuables and Belongings

In the first instance, possibly a letter from a Lawyer could stop them continuing.

- ## The Transfer of Family Property

The Lawyer interviewed on Jump In (the link is on the previous page) suggested four key messages:

> Get Educated
>
> Seek Advice
>
> Monitor Transactions
>
> Never Give Sole Power of Attorney (have a family member you trust implicitly plus your Lawyer or Accountant)

- ## Assets Taken by Caregiver

Another family's story, also shown with the Mickey Rooney interview (the link is on the previous page), tells of how the daughter described how the caregiver took everything her parents had worked all their lives for. Within months of moving in she convinced the elderly father to name her as beneficiary of his estate and disinherit his wife. When they took the matter to Court, The Prosecutor charged the caregiver with various felonies, including theft and forgery.

The Law and How It Views Elder Financial Abuse

- ## Undue Influence Explained (James Kelly, LL.B)

Older people can become vulnerable for many reasons as has been dealt with in the pages you have read in this book. At law there is a doctrine of undue influence.

Undue Influence can occur when a person takes advantage over another person because of the nature of their relationship. That means that one of the parties has some power or authority over the other person and that relationship is exploited. It could be where a person is a carer (or caregiver), or provides assistance to the older person and that person puts pressure on the older person to do something that they succumb to because of the pressure brought to bear or because of the nature of the relationship.

An example of this could be where an older person is badgered into changing their Will, signing over property or makes somebody Power of Attorney because of the influence of the person who is in the dominant position in the relationship.

The Courts are becoming more focused on looking at the evidence where undue influence is alleged against someone who from all appearances was a trusted person in the older person's life.

More Background Information

If you require more information, or to verify the extent that wealth abuse occurs among our elderly, we encourage you to Google key words and your local Law Society, or equivalent in your own State, Country or Province.

You could also Google the following search by keying in words such as:

- Law Society (stating your state, country or province here)
- The Law Society
- Elder Abuse
- Elder Legal Issues
- Undue Influence
- Elder Financial Abuse

A Law Society or the equivalent where you live, in addition to services for Lawyers, they offer services for the Community, such as:

- How can we help you?
- Search Register
- Find a Lawyer or Organisation
- Guides to the Law
- Lawyer's Complaints Service
- Standards Committee decisions
- Lawyer's Fidelity Fund
- Thinking of a Career in Law
- Family Dispute Resolution
- What to consider and what to expect when you see a Lawyer

Important Aspects to Consider

The people who commit these low acts, intent to do so, they do not genuinely care about the wellbeing of the elderly, only getting the money, the assets. They have clandestine ways and are slick operators. They operate "on the sly", and pose as good, caring people. The truth is they will lie and go to great lengths to appear to be innocent and go undetected.

When Undue Influence is used to coerce an elderly or frail and unwitting person, it's considered an abuse. One example: an elderly or frail person could be told "if you don't do this, I'll put you in a nursing home".

In fact, virtually any act of persuasion that overcomes the free will and judgment of another is against the Law. Another example: A young man begins to visit an ageing uncle regularly, the uncle is ill, over time the nephew increasingly urges him to leave his substantial home to him, instead of his son. When at first the old man doesn't agree, the nephew threatens the old man by telling him he's ungrateful, the elderly man is very lonely, the nephew brings over a Lawyer, who does not know the ageing uncle, and is present while he tells the Lawyer to write a new Will in favour of him.

• It's Devastating for Elders

Imagine for a moment how awful these elders must feel, while being coerced in such a way, the loss of dignity, the feelings of uncertainty and being fearful would be huge. Then in addition, if they've been coerced to sign over their assets somehow, the loss of their financial support, their freedom to choose, plus the loss of the inheritance they were going to leave someone, it would all weigh heavily indeed on an elder person.

In addition to knowing how awful this makes an elderly person feel, imagine just how awful you would feel knowing that this occurred to an elder person you love or perhaps even help to care for, and that you either didn't or couldn't say or do anything because you did not know how to or were unsure at the time. What if you tried but were unsuccessful at stepping-in or heading off financial elder abuse. Consider how that would make you feel.

The key to successfully stepping-in, is by not being complacent but to take action. It's all about becoming aware, knowing what to do and how to do it, to step-in and protect the elder or elders you care about. The effort required to step in and help the elders is by far easier than the emotionally devastating effects of when Undue Influence occurs, or as it's appropriately called "The Ultimate Betrayal".

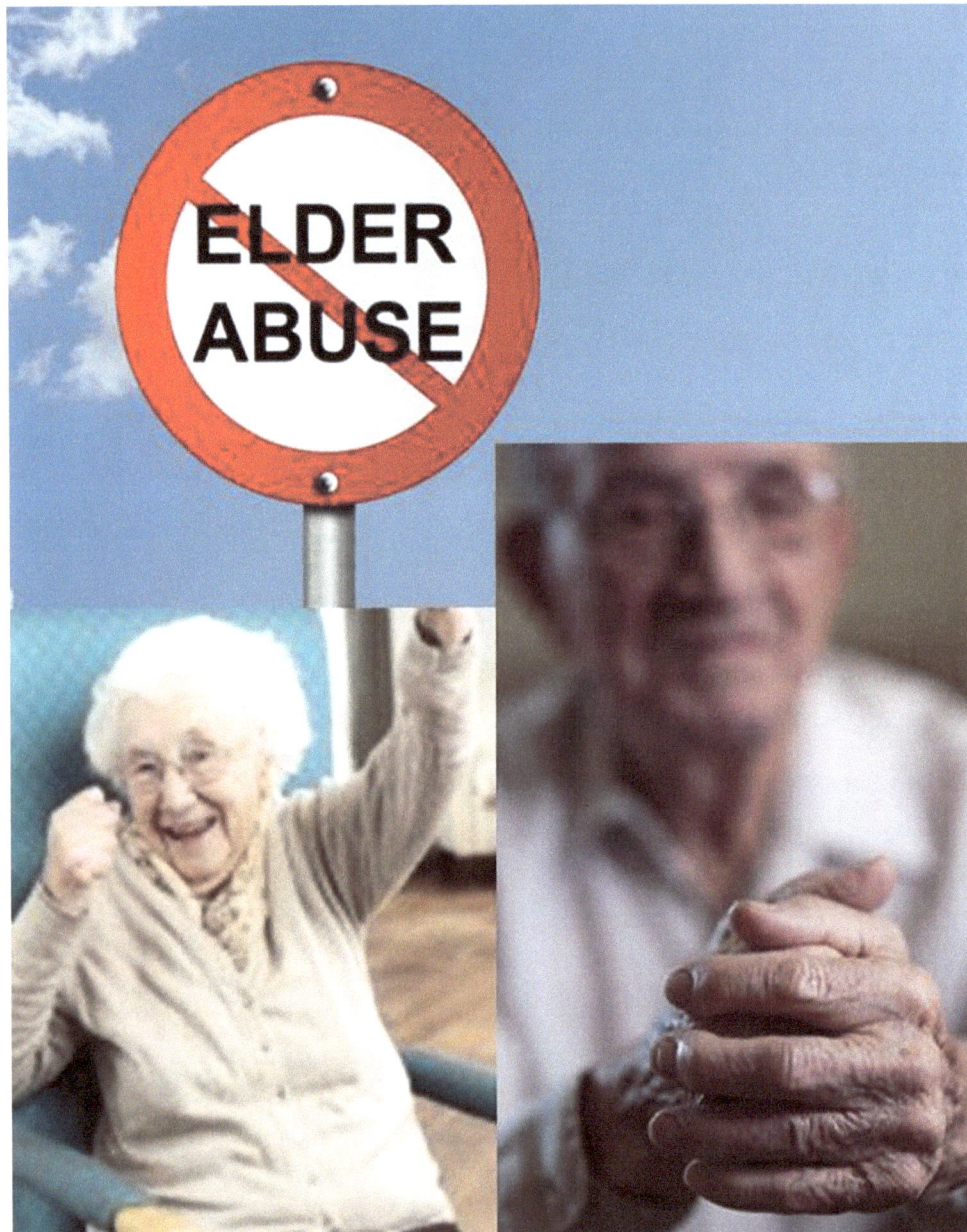

"Yes"!

Your Contacts and Recording Details

• Important to Keep Notes

You can also use this Guide as Your Workbook. In addition you may need a notebook, and consider keeping a Diary, to write all your contacts and their details, plus to keep all your notes in one book.

It's important to consider making notes to remind you of advice and comments.

At some later date you may need to refer to it, as sometimes the process is lengthy and can become complicated. You may find it useful to record as many details as possible, in preparation for a Hearing or for a quick reference.

An example follows:

Lawyer's Contact Phone Number: _____

Lawyer's E-mail Address: _____

Advice/Action Recommended: _____

_____

_____

_____

_____

_____

_____

Other Contacts:_____

_____

_____

_____

_____

_____

_____

_____

Details:_____

_____

_____

_____

_____

_____

_____

Important Things to Note: _____

_____

_____

_____

_____

_____

_____

_____

_____

_____

_____

_____

_____

_____

_____

_____

_____

About the Author
Anne McGowan

Anne is a key speaker at workshops, an author, a writer, and trusted advocate for the elderly. She is the CEO of Protecting Seniors Wealth and firmly believes in creating a better future for our elderly seniors, one where financial abuse and abuse of any kind will be less likely to occur.

Today she uses her skills to create more awareness, to help the many people who have experienced this also and to help prevent it occurring in the future for as many people as possible. For Anne, when she became aware of just how prevalent elder wealth abuse is, it was the catalyst that prompted her to focus now on elder financial abuse prevention.

She brings a successful background in business as a professional qualified public relations consultant where she assisted many high profile people and organisations to communicate their message. Turning those skills now to something important, protecting senior's whole wealth.

Anne enjoys an active life, surrounded by good people and she commends all the great work done by volunteer organisations. Her qualifications, studies and interests include public relations, personal nutrition and fitness, wellness and whole wealth, and personal development.

About Our Consulting Lawyer
James Kelly, LL.B

Qualifications

- Bachelor of Laws
- Diploma Legal Practice
- Notary Public

Year of Admission: 1991

Experience

James studied law at the University of Technology, Sydney while employed as a Parliamentary Officer in the New South Wales Parliament.

He has worked in regional practice since 1991 and has developed his legal practice mainly in the area of "Elder Law". This is the law as it relates to seniors and includes conveyancing, accommodation in facilities such as retirement villages and aged care. He also advises in estate planning from the legal perspective and other general issues affecting older people. He drafts testamentary trusts in Wills and trusts particularly where there are disabled beneficiaries.

James has been employed with Owen Hodge Lawyers since 1995 and became an Associate of the firm in 1996. He was made Partner in July 2000 and is the head of the Seniors, Estates, and Residential Conveyancing team.

James was appointed to the role of Notary Public by the Supreme Court of New South Wales in 2009, and given the statutory power to witness and certify documents, administer oaths and perform other wide-ranging administrative functions of a national and international nature.

James is particularly aware and sensitive to the needs of his clients. He is conscious of the need to communicate with his clients in such a way as to help them make prudent decisions after considering the options.

He is also actively involved with several seniors groups and advisory committees. He also regularly addresses seniors groups on legal issues.

Acknowledgements

Thank you to everyone who has supported the production of this Guide, this important information to help many people head off wealth abuse of our elder members of society.

Perhaps, one the most important aspects of this work, is that it will help keep the dignity of an elder person intact, by informing people of how to protect them. So that the elders will not have to feel fearful and vulnerable, they will not have to experience the fear of the unknown, the uncertainty and the loss of dignity that they feel when they have been taken advantage of financially, when financial abuse or the Ultimate Betrayal takes place, and the perpetrators just don't care.

However, many of us do care, in fact we care a lot. We are concerned about the wellbeing and the respect of our elders.

I would like to say a big thank you to James Kelly, LL.B, for caring enough to take the time out of his busy schedule, to be the Consulting Lawyer and to contribute to the quality of this publication. His input added integrity and it is valued and greatly appreciated.

A big thank you to several key people, for assisting and supporting the idea and the process, they know who they are. Thank you to all the people who offered input and spoke openly of their own experiences, so that we could include examples for people to read. Many are too upset or too embarrassed to include their names, and as a courtesy to them, their names were not included, however their stories are real.

To the many Lawyers who work in the area of Elder Law and do their best to protect seniors and their wealth, I say well done and "good on you" for being diligent and for "looking out" for the client's best interests.

To all the people who take a stand, and do something, those who speak up and step in to help elders where and when the need arises. I'm certain the many millions of elders internationally who are adversely affected and lose billions of dollars every year due to financial abuse, would thank you as well, if they could.

Perhaps those elders, if they were able to speak in a stronger or louder voice, they would say something similar to the following quote.

I would thank you from the bottom of my heart,
but for you my heart has no bottom.

      – Unknown

MY NOTES

www.ingramcontent.com/pod-product-compliance
Lightning Source LLC
Chambersburg PA
CBHW052043190326
41520CB00002BA/170